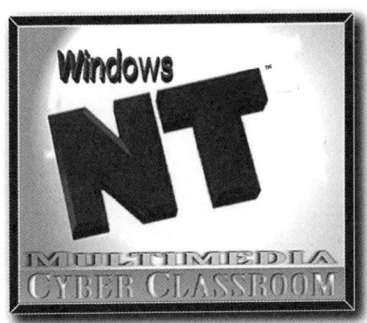

User Guide

Prentice Hall PTR
Upper Saddle River, NJ 07458
http://www.phptr.com

© 1998 by Prentice Hall PTR
Prentice-Hall, Inc.
A Simon & Schuster Company
Upper Saddle River, NJ 07458

Prentice Hall books are widely used by corporations and government agencies for training, marketing, and resale.

All products or services mentioned in this book are the trademarks or service marks of their respective companies or organizations.

Printed in the United States of America
10 9 8 7 6 5 4 3 2 1

ISBN   0-13-081646-9

Prentice-Hall International (UK) Limited, *London*
Prentice-Hall of Australia Pty. Limited, *Sydney*
Prentice-Hall Canada Inc., *Toronto*
Prentice-Hall Hispanoamericana, S.A., *Mexico*
Prentice-Hall of India Private Limited, *New Delhi*
Prentice-Hall of Japan, Inc., *Tokyo*
Simon & Schuster Asia Pte. Ltd., *Singapore*
Editora Prentice-Hall do Brasil, Ltda., *Rio de Janeiro*

Contents

System Requirements

Thank you for purchasing the *Windows NT Multimedia Cyber Classroom* from Prentice Hall PTR Interactive. Because the Cyber Classroom is written in Java™, it requires a system that supports the 1.1 version of the Java Virtual Machine. Before installing the Cyber Classroom, be sure that your system meets the following minimum requirements:

Operating System

The Cyber Classroom will run under Microsoft Windows® 95, Windows® 98, or Windows NT™ 4.0 or higher. The memory requirements for the Cyber Classroom are 16 MB RAM for Windows 95 and 98, and 32 MB RAM for Windows NT.

Disk Space

The "Typical" installation option requires 20 MB free disk space. The "Optimized for Performance" installation option copies all of the data files to your hard disk and requires approximately 200 MB free disk space.

Sound Card

SoundBlaster, SoundBlaster Pro, SoundBlaster Pro 16, and all Sound-Blaster compatibles.

CD-ROM Drive

Four-speed CD-ROM drive and higher.

Video

SVGA and compatible. The Cyber Classroom is designed to run at a resolution of 640 x 480 in 256 colors. Higher resolutions generally work fine.

Installing and Removing the Cyber Classroom

Installing the Cyber Classroom

Insert the CD-ROM into your drive and run the program *setup.exe,* which is in the CD's root directory. *setup.exe* takes you through a series of dialog boxes. After viewing the initial "Welcome" dialog box, click *Next* to see the Destination dialog box:

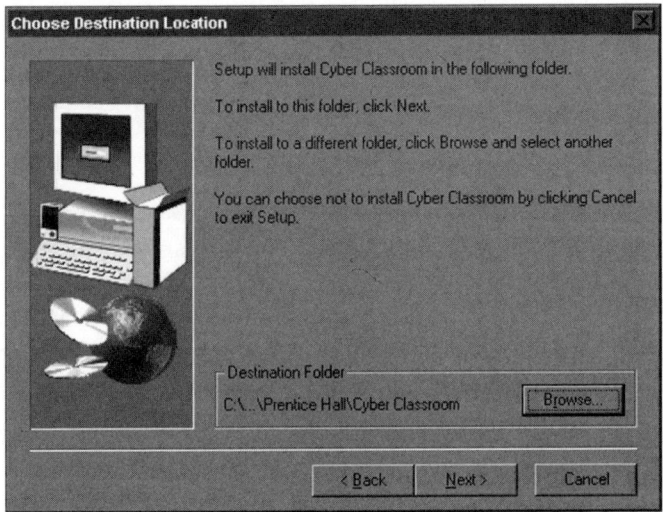

If you want to change the default location, click the *Browse* button. When the Destination Folder displays the location you want, click the *Next* button to move to the Setup dialog box:

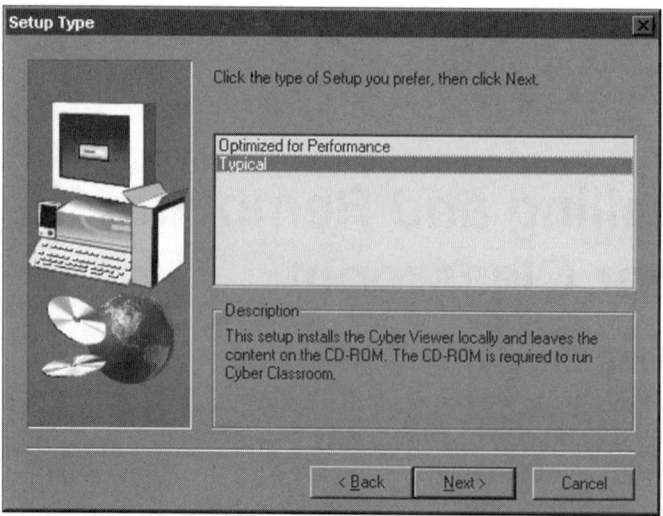

You have two installation options: "Typical" and "Optimized for Performance." The "Typical" option places the Cyber Classroom viewer and the Java Virtual Machine on your hard disk and leaves all of the data files on the CD-ROM. To run the Cyber Classroom, you must keep the CD-ROM in the CD-ROM drive.

The "Optimized for Performance" option copies all of the data files to your hard disk along with the viewer and virtual machine. You do not need to keep the CD-ROM in the CD-ROM drive to run it. Because there is a great deal of digital movie data on the CD-ROM, you need approximately 200 MB of free disk space if you choose this option. For most users, the "Typical" installation option works just fine.

Click *Next* to move to the Program Folder dialog box:

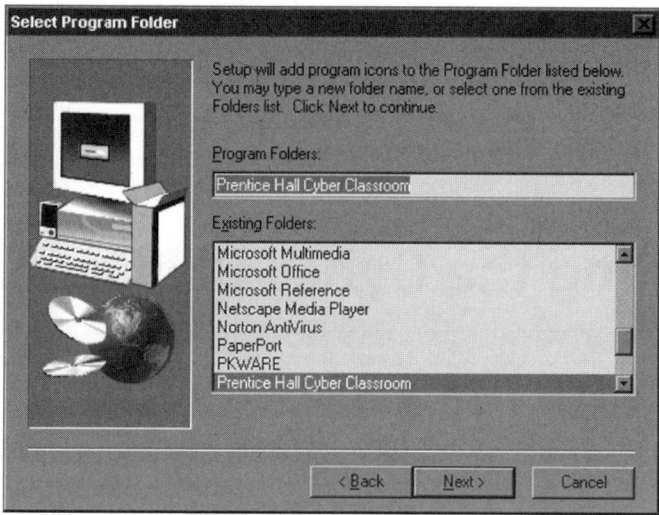

You can accept either the default program folder name or select another folder name, then click *Next* one more time.

The installation of the *Windows NT Multimedia Cyber Classroom* is complete.

Removing the Cyber Classroom

You can remove the Cyber Classroom through the Windows Control Panel. To do so, click the *Add/Remove* icon in the Control Panel, highlight "Windows NT Multimedia Cyber Classroom," then click the *Add/Remove* button.

The Cyber Classroom is removed after you confirm that you want it removed.

Starting the Cyber Classroom

Start Here!

Start the Cyber Classroom by selecting the *Windows NT Multimedia Cyber Classroom* icon in the *Prentice Hall Cyber Classroom* program group available from the *Start* button.

The first time you start the Cyber Classroom, the *Home Page* is displayed.

Home Page

Click the *About the Authors* icon to find out about John Deep and Ed Kear. Next, click the *Introduction* icon. Like all Prentice Hall PTR Interactive Multimedia Cyber Classroom products, this CD-ROM contains a multimedia slide show that presents a general overview of the wealth of resources available to you in the Cyber Classroom. Be sure to view this introduction to find out how these resources will help you learn how to administer Windows NT Server 4.0. Then, finally, click the *Table of Contents* icon to access the hot-linked Table of Contents.

The installation program installs the *Windows NT Multimedia Cyber Classroom Web Page* on your system. Open the web page by clicking on its icon in the *Prentice Hall Cyber Classroom* program group. This web page contains a *README* section that includes up-to-date information about the Cyber Classroom. It also includes the multimedia slide show introductions for the other five Prentice Hall PTR Interactive Cyber Classrooms. You can watch them in your browser to find out about the other Cyber Classrooms.

You also need to know how to get around in the Cyber Classroom. We have provided navigation tools that move you from one screen to another, from one section to another, and from chapter to another. Read about these very useful tools in **"Navigating Through the Cyber Classroom,"** the next section in this User Guide.

Exiting the Cyber Classroom

Click "File" on the menu bar, then click "Exit" and the Cyber Classroom closes.

Note: When you restart the Cyber Classroom, it will open where you were when you last left it.

Navigating Through the Cyber Classroom

The *Windows NT Multimedia Cyber Classroom* includes several powerful navigation tools which take you from screen to screen, section to section, and chapter to chapter.

Navigation Tools

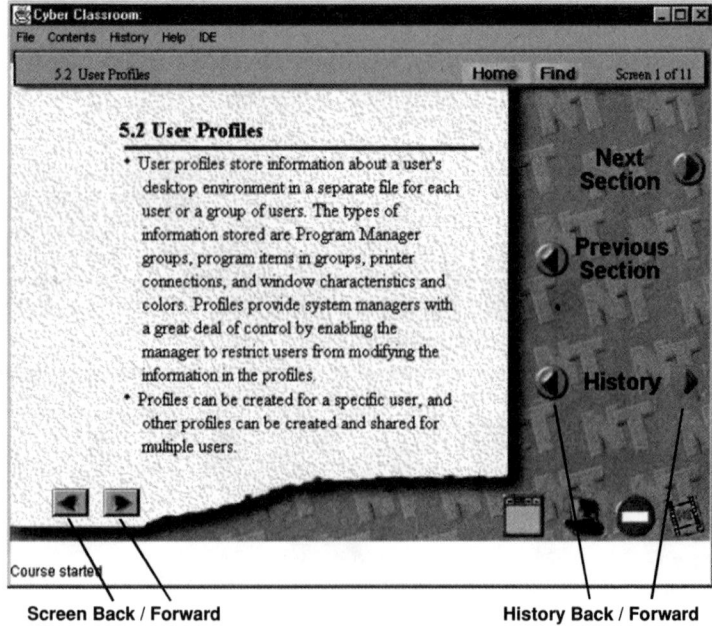

Screen Back / Forward   History Back / Forward

Screen Forward Button

Use the right-pointing red button in the lower-left corner of the screen to move forward one screen. When you arrive at the last screen of a section, this button takes you to the first screen of the next section.

Screen Back Button

Use the left-pointing red button in the lower-left corner of the screen to move back one screen. When you arrive at the first screen of a section, this button takes you to the last screen of the previous section.

Previous/Next Section Buttons

The shaded column on the right of the screen contains buttons that link to the beginning of the section immediately preceding or immediately following the current section. Click on the appropriate button to move backward or forward by section.

History Back/Forward Buttons

The two red buttons next to "History" in the shaded column on the right allow you to retrace your steps. Click the left-pointing red button to move back through the places you've been in the Cyber Classroom. Click the right-pointing red button to retrace your steps forward in this list.

History Menu Item

The "History" menu item also allows you to retrace your steps. Click "History" on the menu bar and select a place to return to from the drop-down list. You will find these "History" features very useful when you want to return to a place in the Cyber Classroom.

Contents Menu Item

The "Contents" menu item provides several ways to move through the Cyber Classroom. Click "Contents" on the menu bar and select a chapter from the drop-down list. The first page that you jump to is the outline for that chapter. Click a section title to jump to that section.

Within any given chapter, click "Contents" on the menu bar, then "Current Chapter." A cascading menu appears that lists the sections in that chapter. Click a section title to jump to that section.

Find Button

The Cyber Classroom contains a powerful, full-text search engine. Click the *Find* button at the top of the screen to start a Text Search. Enter the topic you are looking for in the "Enter Text To Search For" field of the Text Search dialog box. Double-click on a topic in the alphabetical list that appears in the "Narrow Your Search" window. A list of "hits" appears in the window below the "Go To The Relevant Section" button. You can go to one of the relevant sections by either double-clicking on a section in the list, or by highlighting the section and then clicking on the "Go To The Relevant Section" button.

The hits are ranked in order of relevancy to the topic you entered in the text search field. Select the "Sort by Order of Appearance" option to rank the hits in the order that they appear in the Cyber Classroom.

Click on the *Previous* and *Next* buttons to continue viewing the screens of the selected section, and to view the other relevant sections in the ranking order you selected.

Home Button

Click the *Home* button at the top of the screen to jump to the *Home Page*. The *Home Page* contains links to information about the authors, the Table of Contents, and a multimedia slide show introduction that presents an overview of the Cyber Classroom.

Understanding Chapter Organization

The *Windows NT Multimedia Cyber Classroom* is organized into chapters. Each chapter has the following components:

Outline

At the beginning of each chapter is an outline. This outline contains hot links to each section in the chapter.

Objectives

Click the *Objectives* icon at the bottom of the outline screen to view the chapter's objectives. Then click the *Speaker* icon in the chapter's objectives window to hear one of the authors describe what you are going to learn in that chapter.

Sections

Each chapter has multiple sections consisting of text, illustrations, tips, common errors, digital movies, and hot links to other sections relevant to the current section. Icons in the left margin of the text and hot links within the text itself provide access to these features. In addition, there is a palette of special features icons at the bottom of each screen. These icons open windows that display the illustrations, tips, common errors, and digital movies for that chapter. The special features icons are described in **"Linking to Special Features,"** the next section in this User Guide.

Typical Section Screen

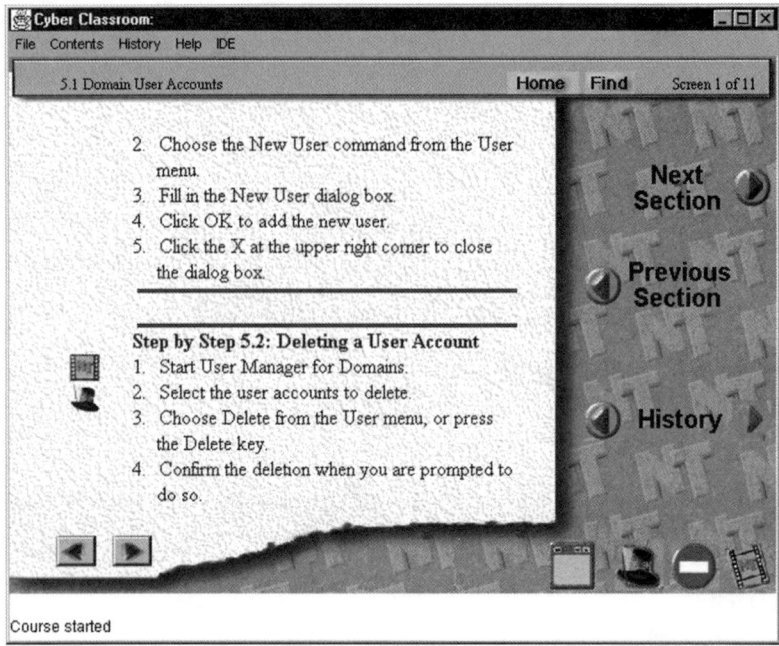

Interactive Exercises

There are interactive exercises at the end of each chapter to test your understanding of key procedures introduced in that chapter. They are fill-in-the-blank, true or false, and multiple choice questions. For the fill-in-the-blank exercises, drag the option you think correctly completes the sentence into the blank. Then click the *Check Your Answer* button. For the true or false and multiple choice questions, check the option you think correctly answers the question. Then click the *Check Your Answer* button.

The Cyber Classroom lets you try as many times as you like to get the right answer and offers helpful comments as you do the exercises.

Fill-in-the-Blank Exercise

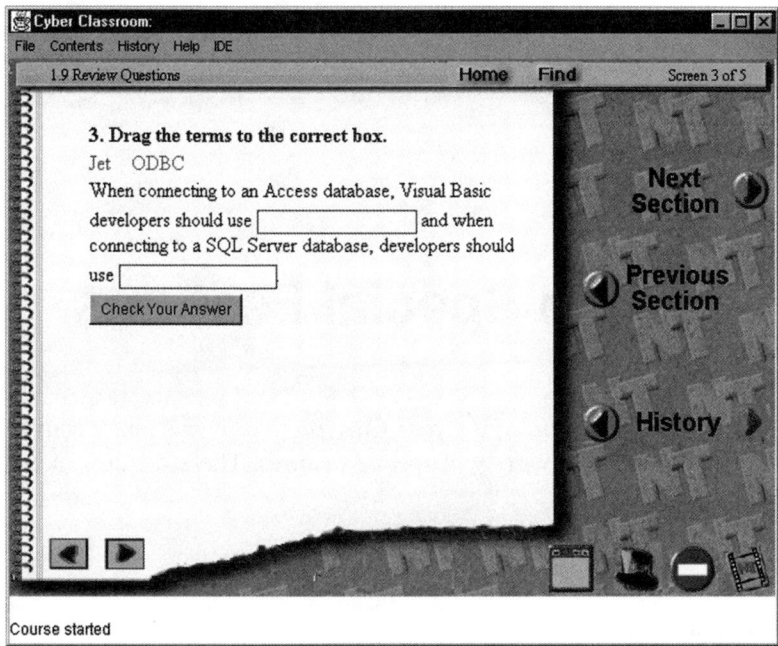

Digital Movies

The Cyber Classroom contains 250 digital movies that demonstrate key NT administration tasks, step-by-step. As you watch, NT experts John Deep and Ed Kear describe the procedure and explain the reasoning behind each technique. The digital movies are described in detail in **"Linking to Special Features,"** the next section in this User Guide.

Linking to Special Features

The *Windows NT Multimedia Cyber Classroom* provides many convenient ways to access a variety of special features. These features include:

- illustrations
- tips and tricks
- common errors
- digital movies
- interactive exercises

Icons for these features appear in the left margin of the text and along the bottom of the screen. Click a text margin icon to display an illustration, tip, common error, or digital movie that is germane to that particular text. Click one of the icons at the bottom of the screen to access hot links to the illustrations, or view the tips, common errors, or digital movies for the current chapter. These icons are shown and described in detail below.

Special Features Icons

Objectives

Click the *Objectives* icon at the bottom of the chapter's outline screen to open the objectives window. Click the *Speaker* in the objectives window to listen to one of the authors describe what you are going to learn in that chapter. Continue moving through the objectives by clicking the right- and left-pointing buttons in the window.

Illustrations

Click the *Illustrations* icon in the bottom-right corner of the screen to open a window displaying a hot-linked list of the current chapter's illustrations. Click to view the first one and then continue moving through the illustrations by clicking the right- and left-pointing buttons in the window.

The *Illustrations* icon also appears in the left margin of the text to show you an illustration relevant to that section.

Wizard Tips

Click the *Wizard Tips* icon in the bottom-right corner of the screen to open a window displaying a hot-linked list of the current chapter's tips and tricks. These tips describe techniques for maximizing NT's performance. Click to view the first one and then continue viewing these tips and tricks by clicking the right- and left-pointing buttons in the window.

The *Wizard Tips* icon also appears in the left margin of the text to show you a tip or trick relevant to that section.

Common Errors

Click the *Common Errors* icon in the bottom-right corner of the screen to open a window displaying a hot-linked list of the current chapter's *Warnings*. The insights in this window will help you avoid trouble. Click to view the first one and then continue viewing the *Warnings* by clicking the right- and left-pointing buttons in the window.

The *Common Errors* icon also appears in the left margin of the text to show you a *Warning* relevant to that section.

Digital Movies

Click the *Digital Movie* icon in the bottom-right corner of the screen to open a window displaying a hot-linked list of the current chapter's digital movies. When you click on a movie title, you go to the place in the Cyber Classroom where it occurs. Click the *Digital Movie* icon in the text margin to start the movie. The control bar at the bottom of the movie screen allows you to pause, restart, rewind, fast forward, or stop the movie. The digital movie window closes when it is finished playing.

Digital Movie Screen

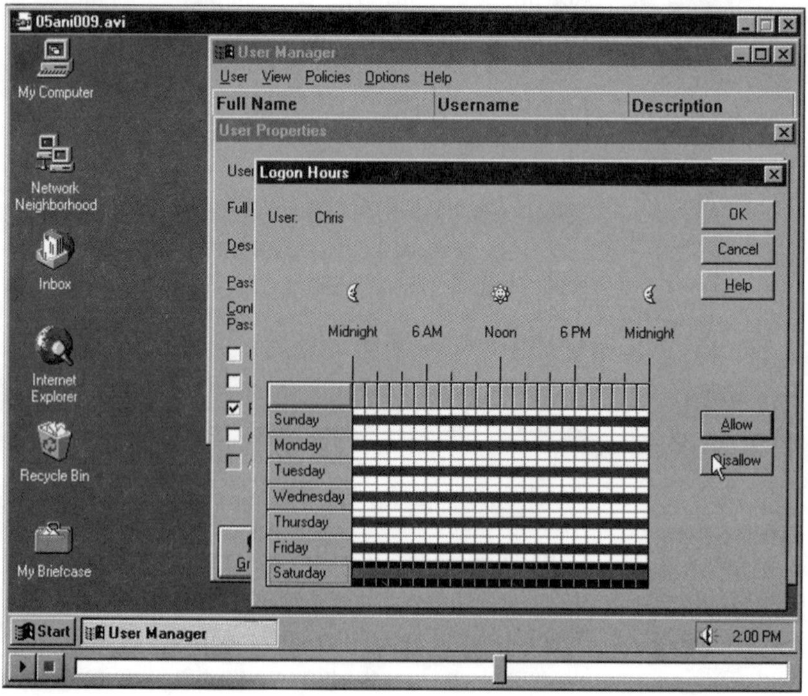

The digital movies are .avi files, and they are played with the Media Player that ships with Windows. The window containing the movies will appear at the screen coordinates at which you last played an .avi file in the Media Player. If the movies appear partially offscreen when you click the *Digital Movie* icon in the Cyber Classroom, do the following:

1. Quit the Cyber Classroom.

2. Launch the Media Player as a stand-alone application. A shortcut to the Media Player is typically located in the Programs -> Accessories -> Multimedia menu available from the Windows Start button.

3. Position the digital movie screen where you want the movies to appear. This would typically be towards the top of your screen, and towards the left. Move the Media Player control window so that it is accessible while the movie is playing.

4. Load any of the .avi files located on the CD-ROM in the WINNT directory into the Media Player.

5. When the file finishes playing, select File -> Close from the Media Player, then quit the Media Player.

6. Restart the Cyber Classroom. When you click on any of the digital movie icons, the movies will open where you closed the .avi file in the Media Player.

Getting Technical Support

If you have software problems, check the *README* portion of the web page. If you don't find an answer for your problem in the *README*, point your browser to the Prentice Hall PTR Interactive Web Site—*http://www.phptr.com*. A link to this site is provided on the web page.

If you continue to experience difficulties, call (201) 236-3477 between 9:00 am and 4:00 pm Eastern Time, Monday through Friday.

Our technical support staff will need to know certain things about your system in order to help solve your problems quickly and efficiently. If possible, please be at your computer when you call for support. You should have the following information ready:

- Product title and product ISBN (this information is on the package)
- Computer make and model
- CD-ROM drive make and model
- RAM available
- Hard disk space available
- Graphics card type
- Sound card type
- Detailed description of the problem, including the exact wording of any error messages

You can also report a software problem by sending an e-mail to *tech_support@prenhall.com*. Along with all the information listed above, be sure to include a telephone number where you can be reached.

LICENSE AGREEMENT

YOU SHOULD CAREFULLY READ THE FOLLOWING TERMS AND CONDITIONS BEFORE BREAKING THE SEAL ON THE PACKAGE. AMONG OTHER THINGS, THIS AGREEMENT LICENSES THE ENCLOSED SOFTWARE TO YOU AND CONTAINS WARRANTY AND LIABILITY DISCLAIMERS. BY BREAKING THE SEAL ON THE PACKAGE, YOU ARE ACCEPTING AND AGREEING TO THE TERMS AND CONDITIONS OF THIS AGREEMENT. IF YOU DO NOT AGREE TO THE TERMS OF THIS AGREEMENT, DO NOT BREAK THE SEAL. YOU SHOULD PROMPTLY RETURN THE PACKAGE UNOPENED.

LICENSE.

Subject to the provisions contained herein, Prentice-Hall, Inc. ("PH") hereby grants to you a non-exclusive, non-transferable license to use the object code version of the computer software product ("Software") contained in the package on a single computer of the type identified on the package.

SOFTWARE AND DOCUMENTATION.

PH shall furnish the Software to you on media in machine-readable object code form and may also provide the standard documentation ("Documentation") containing instructions for operation and use of the Software.

LICENSE TERM AND CHARGES.

The term of this license commences upon delivery of the Software to you and is perpetual unless earlier terminated upon default or as otherwise set forth herein.

TITLE.

Title, and ownership right, and intellectual property rights in and to the Software and Documentation shall remain in PH and/or in suppliers to PH of programs contained in the Software. The Software is provided for your own internal use under this license. This license does not include the right to sublicense and is personal to you and therefore may not be assigned (by operation of law or otherwise) or transferred without the prior written consent of PH. You acknowledge that the Software in source code form remains a confidential trade secret of PH and/or its suppliers and therefore you agree not to attempt to decipher or decompile, modify, disassemble, reverse engineer or prepare derivative works of the Software or develop source code for the Software or knowingly allow others to do so. Further, you may not copy the Documentation or other written materials accompanying the Software.

UPDATES.

This license does not grant you any right, license, or interest in and to any improvements, modifications, enhancements, or updates to the Software and Documentation. Updates, if available, may be obtained by you at PH's then current standard pricing, terms, and conditions.

LIMITED WARRANTY AND DISCLAIMER.

PH warrants that the media containing the Software, if provided by PH, is free from defects in material and workmanship under normal use for a period of sixty (60) days from the date you purchased a license to it.

THIS IS A LIMITED WARRANTY AND IT IS THE ONLY WARRANTY MADE BY PH. THE SOFTWARE IS PROVIDED 'AS IS' AND PH SPECIFICALLY DISCLAIMS ALL WARRANTIES OF ANY KIND, EITHER EXPRESS OR IMPLIED, INCLUDING, BUT NOT LIMITED TO, THE IMPLIED WARRANTY OF MERCHANTABILITY AND FITNESS FOR A PARTICULAR PURPOSE. FURTHER, COMPANY DOES NOT WARRANT, GUARANTY OR MAKE ANY REPRESENTATIONS REGARDING THE USE, OR THE RESULTS OF THE USE, OF THE SOFTWARE IN TERMS OF COR-RECTNESS, ACCURACY, RELIABILITY, CURRENTNESS, OR OTHERWISE AND DOES NOT WARRANT THAT THE OPERATION OF ANY SOFTWARE WILL BE UNINTERRUPTED OR ERROR FREE. COMPANY EXPRESSLY DISCLAIMS ANY WARRANTIES NOT STATED HEREIN. NO ORAL OR WRITTEN INFORMATION OR ADVICE GIVEN BY PH, OR ANY PH DEALER, AGENT, EMPLOYEE OR OTHERS SHALL CREATE, MODIFY OR EXTEND A WARRANTY OR IN ANY WAY INCREASE THE SCOPE OF THE FOREGOING WARRANTY, AND NEITHER SUBLICENSEE OR PURCHASER MAY RELY ON ANY SUCH INFORMATION OR ADVICE. If the media is subjected to accident, abuse, or improper use; or if you violate the terms of this Agreement, then this warranty shall immediately be terminated. This warranty shall not apply if the Software is used on or in conjunction with hardware or programs other than the unmodified version of hardware and programs with which the Software was designed to be used as described in the Documentation.

LIMITATION OF LIABILITY.

Your sole and exclusive remedies for any damage or loss in any way connected with the Software are set forth below. UNDER NO CIRCUMSTANCES AND UNDER NO LEGAL THEORY, TORT, CONTRACT, OR OTHERWISE, SHALL PH BE LIABLE TO YOU OR ANY OTHER PERSON FOR ANY INDIRECT, SPECIAL, INCIDENTAL, OR CONSEQUENTIAL DAMAGES OF ANY CHARACTER INCLUDING, WITHOUT LIMITATION, DAMAGES FOR LOSS OF GOODWILL, LOSS OF PROFIT, WORK STOPPAGE, COMPUTER FAILURE OR MALFUNCTION, OR ANY AND ALL OTHER COMMERCIAL DAMAGES OR LOSSES, OR FOR ANY OTHER DAMAGES EVEN IF PH SHALL HAVE BEEN INFORMED OF THE POSSIBILITY OF SUCH DAMAGES, OR FOR ANY CLAIM BY ANY OTHER PARTY. PH'S THIRD PARTY PROGRAM SUPPLIERS MAKE NO WARRANTY, AND HAVE NO LIABILITY WHATSOEVER, TO YOU. PH's sole and exclusive obligation and liability and your exclusive remedy shall be: upon PH's election, (i) the replacement of your defective media; or (ii) the repair or correction of your defective media if PH is able, so that it will conform to the above warranty; or (iii) if PH is unable to replace or repair, you may terminate this license by returning the Software. Only if you inform PH of your problem during the appli-cable warranty period will PH be obligated to honor this warranty. You may contact PH to inform PH of the problem as follows:

SOME STATES OR JURISDICTIONS DO NOT ALLOW THE EXCLUSION OF IMPLIED WARRANTIES OR LIMITATION OR EXCLUSION OF CONSEQUENTIAL DAMAGES, SO THE ABOVE LIMITATIONS OR EXCLUSIONS MAY NOT APPLY TO YOU. THIS WARRANTY GIVES YOU SPECIFIC LEGAL RIGHTS AND YOU MAY ALSO HAVE OTHER RIGHTS WHICH VARY BY STATE OR JURISDICTION.

MISCELLANEOUS.

If any provision of this Agreement is held to be ineffective, unenforceable, or illegal under certain circumstances for any reason, such decision shall not affect the validity or enforceability (i) of such provision under other circumstances or (ii) of the remaining provisions hereof under all circumstances and such provision shall be reformed to and only to the extent necessary to make it effective, enforceable, and legal under such circumstances. All headings are solely for convenience and shall not be considered in interpreting this Agreement. This Agreement shall be governed by and construed under New York law as such law applies to agreements between New York residents entered into and to be performed entirely within New York, except as required by U.S. Government rules and regulations to be governed by Federal law.

YOU ACKNOWLEDGE THAT YOU HAVE READ THIS AGREEMENT, UNDERSTAND IT, AND AGREE TO BE BOUND BY ITS TERMS AND CONDITIONS. YOU FURTHER AGREE THAT IT IS THE COMPLETE AND EXCLUSIVE STATEMENT OF THE AGREEMENT BETWEEN US THAT SUPERSEDES ANY PROPOSAL OR PRIOR AGREEMENT, ORAL OR WRITTEN, AND ANY OTHER COMMUNICATIONS BETWEEN US RELATING TO THE SUBJECT MATTER OF THIS AGREEMENT.

U.S. GOVERNMENT RESTRICTED RIGHTS.

Use, duplication or disclosure by the Government is subject to restrictions set forth in subparagraphs (a) through (d) of the Commercial Computer-Restricted Rights clause at FAR 52.227-19 when applicable, or in subparagraph (c) (1) (ii) of the Rights in Technical Data and Computer Software clause at DFARS 252.227-7013, and in similar clauses in the NASA FAR Supplement.